Embracing

The Queen Within

Embracing The Queen Within

Discovering My Identity

Melody Saunders

Melody Saunders
Atlanta, Georgia

Published by:

Melody Saunders
Atlanta, GA

Published in the United States of America.

ISBN 978-0-578-53223-3

Contents

Preface

Embracing the Queen Within is a book that helps to rediscover the purpose of ones' existence and seize hold of what God has for you. This book will help you to face your past, walk in your present, and embrace your future. This book opened my eyes to see that life is much more than just existing but living. It is not only just living carelessly but living with a purpose, for a purpose, and on purpose. Many times, we walk around thinking that God is mad at us or that God does not want anything to do with us. But that is not the case He is just waiting for us to acknowledge Him in all our ways so that He can direct our path. He also promised to never leave us nor forsake us. He is all the while trying to get us to align ourselves back up with the purpose for which He specifically called us to fulfill.

There is no way that He can walk away from us unless we turn away from Him. Throughout my life I found out that He was there all the time. He does not force

Himself on us or His ways upon us but gives us free will. In doing so we can come to discover on our own the need for Him and His will for our lives. In walking out life I discovered more the need for Him in my life and realized that if it was not for Him, I would not make it and overcome the many trials that I face in life. So, Embracing the Queen Within book is just that testimony of how I overcame the temptations and trials and found my way back to God and a deeper relationship with Him. By the end of this book I hope that your faith will be stronger and that your relationship with Him be restored and even deeper than before. For I learned and am reminded of Isaiah 55:8-9: For my thoughts are not your thoughts, neither are your ways my ways, declares the Lord. For as the heavens are higher than the earth, so are my ways higher than your ways and my thoughts than your thoughts.

Through this book, you will find salvation, hope, freedom, and deliverance from life's obstacle to walk into your destiny. I would like to thank my parents and husband who always encouraged me to be the best me and pour out what God has placed on the inside of me. Also, to my children who helped me discover my strengths when I did not even know they existed. I am truly blessed.

Introduction

Depression, Loneliness, Hopelessness, and Rejection are reactants that can lead us down a path of destruction. If we don't catch and take heed to what is causing these things, they can make us fall prey to the tactics of the enemy; therefore, allowing all kinds of toxins that can consume our mind, body, and soul and possibly lead to disease, sickness, mental disorders, and even suicide. It is easy to blame others for our challenges instead of taking responsibility and internalizing the choices that we make. The beauty of this life is having choices. God does not force anything on us but makes everything available to us. The choices we make when challenged can lead us down a path of life or destruction causing us to either reflect or distort the image God originally designed for us to carry into the world. Reflecting His image comes with a benefits package that leads to a life of peace, joy, and a sound mind. The decision, however, is left up to us.

We all have done things that have led us down paths that caused us pain, loneliness, and disappointment. But these by-products are not designed to forever be holding cells. Instead they are designed to be learning blocks that help us to grow and develop into the full image of our Heavenly Father's desire. Our Godly reflection will not only depict our brokenness but the picture of how we were repaired into beautiful butterflies. However, when we don't take the opportunity to reconnect to the Heavenly Father, who is the true giver of life, it opens the door to dwelling in depression, loneliness, and hopelessness. Instead of learning how to embrace His Word in order to conquer the toxins that try to consume us through the tests of life, we have conformed to the pattern of this world. God never promised that this walk was going to be easy or that there would be no challenges in this life. But He gave us an illustration through Jesus Christ to demonstrate that despite being in this flesh we can still walk upright.

Toxins that can pollute us are not only drugs, alcohol, and sex outside of marriage, but a lack of confidence, negative talking, and low self-esteem. These are danger signs. Warnings to go in the opposite direction. These signs are a cry for help because they can lead to depression, even suicide. But this book will enlighten, empower, and assist you with Embracing the Queen that is on the inside of you!!!

Reflections

12

Chapter I

How Did I Get Here?

Life's schedules and deadlines that seem to occur on a day to day basis can easily conform us into walking zombies. We no longer have an identity but fall prey to the tactics of the enemy and allow the systems of this world to make us into robots. We are locked into rituals instead of pursuing our callings and living out our dreams.

Therefore, the results of not seeking out and pursuing God's way of doing things, we seek for worldly acceptance and foolish deception of success that we think means fame. Our unwillingness to surrender our lives causes us to run away from the image God truly designed for us to be. Why do we do this and what can we do to change this hypocrisy?

There is a mirror in our mind that creates a reflection from what we are internalizing through our ear gates, eye gates and spirit. This reflection can be a distorted image if we do not uphold and meditate foremost on the truth found in the Word of God. The picture that the world most of the time paints for us is contrary and conflicts with the Godly image from the Word of God; yet, we fail to realize that we possess the power to control that which we internalize within our own mind. We give too much of power over to the enemy. We must take back our power and utilize it to help us to walk out the true purpose for which God created for us to be and perform before the foundation of the world.

A great illustration of this is Jeremiah 1:5 (AMP). Although God was speaking to Jeremiah, we can take this text and apply it to our own selves to understand that we were all created specifically for a purpose. God wants us to take into thought that the image of Him will be displayed when we take the time to discover our purpose for which He created for us to perform here in the Earth by building a relationship with Him through studying of His Word. Therefore, the world's image will not be as appealing because of our discovery of the uniqueness and greatness that we see will satisfy us and busy us with His purpose.

On the road of discovery of this purpose we cross different paths and endure different tests. These paths may appear as suffering and lonely but are grounds for strengthening and pruning. This is all preparing us for the purpose for which we were called to by God.

As we walk through these unforeseen paths that may appear as intimidating circumstances and excruciatingly painful, we receive a new revelation of God and what He wants us to do so that we can walk out our purpose on the Earth.

It is in these challenging moments on our journey we must rely heavily on the Word such as found in Romans 8:28 (AMP): And we know [with great confidence] that God [who is deeply concerned about us] causes all things to work together [as a plan] for good for those who love God, to those who are called according to His plan and purpose.

As well as embrace our identity as kingdom citizens and our image of beauty and strength, instead of walking around lost; wearing masks that hide our true identities and recreating ourselves in the image everyone else thinks we should be instead of what God says about us. In this big world where people are competing in their businesses and greed is ruining lives, many have started walking away from God and are left feeling insecure, empty, suicidal and fearful.

I was one who would always compare my life to others. I looked at everyone else as more appealing, more popular, and more intelligent than me. I questioned myself and ability creating a picture of what I think I should look to please others in order to draw attention. But I found out that the attention I drew was not what it all appeared to be or worth me belittling myself to become. As much as I tried, there was not enough or an end to meeting up to the worldly standards. My appearance was unique, my ideas were not popular, and my attitude just seemed too proper. As much as we can try to conform to the image, it will never be enough, it will not work because we were born to stand out. There will always be something about you that will not meet to their ideal standard. It is not until we become who God created us to become will we become satisfied and successful.

There is a mark that Christ puts on you especially when you are anointed by God, there is no hiding it. It doesn't matter where you run or how you try to change your appearance, it is like a light that will never die.

It shines and everywhere you go others just leave you alone because you carry something so special that it is not meant to defy. Some men flee, some friends depart, and some things never work out because the magnitude of the anointing on your life shields you from the darkness and brutal acts that can take many people out.

There were times that I wanted to give up because I didn't understand and moments when I made bad decisions because I was not aware of God's plan. Although there are consequences and judgments we must face for our inadequate decisions, God's grace sustains us during these times and gets us back on track after we repent and turn back to Him. This is what happened to me. After acknowledging my falling away, it was like God immediately forgave me and presented me another opportunity as if I never walked away from Him. Yet still showing me the error of my way but in a less excruciating way. I learned in the process to be obedient when He speaks to avoid the consequences that accompany harmful decisions, therefore not taking advantage of His grace. But understanding how we can infringe our disobedience on others. Therefore, unaware of the hurt that is laid on others and burdens on which they are left carrying.

I am reminded of the story of Jonah. God told him to go to Nineveh, but he fled to Tarshis. Well, a storm came, and the ship was in danger. Everyone cast lots and the lot fell upon Jonah; he urged them to throw him overboard. He knew that it was him that caused this great storm to stir. But God had a plan and allowed a whale to swallow him up for three days and nights. It was not until he cried out to the Lord and prayed for God to forgive him that he was spit out of the mouth of the whale.

Another demonstration of the grace and plan of God, there was a girl named Hadassah (Esther), an orphan whose mother and father died. She didn't have the opportunity to be raised by her mother and father but was being raised by her cousin. Although her upbringing was not one that she may have desired to the death of the two most precious individuals in a child's life, they may have left her feeling empty and unfit being called into the palace. We can all relate to Esther in that we too have wished that things in our lives were a little different or had gone a different way. There are many questions we ask like, "Why?" However, it is not our goal to answer those questions but to keep living and allow God to reveal and use them as He will to show us His omniscience. Everything in our life that happens forms apart of completing a puzzle that comes together to create the most beautiful picture.

Some of us try so hard to deny our identity and forget our past that we don't realize that it made us who we are and created the strength and beauty that we possess inside. We are so busy looking and living through others that we forget how God made us. Psalms 139:14 (AMP) says, "I will give thanks and praise to You, for I am fearfully and wonderfully made; Wonderful are Your works, And my soul knows it very well."

Even though Esther grew up with her cousin as her guardian, it didn't prevent her from becoming the next Queen. Her confidence, relentlessness, and beauty from her path that she was given by God to ensure that she would be groomed into the wonderful woman soon to be Queen that she was that made her outshine and receive such an outpouring of favor that made the other ladies even love her.

She was before the foundation of the world created to walk through this and all she had to do was obey the eunuch and her cousin to ensure that it was manifested in the Earth realm. She was willing and obedient and surrendered over to the will of the Father therefore God carried her all the way and completed the promise to her. She sacrificed her own will and prayed and fasted to ensure that the lives of her people and not just herself was secure. She exposed herself and risked her life and the throne to ensure that her people's lives were spared. She performed a sacrifice close to the Son of God. But hers was not unto death which made this story a great example of surrendering, obedience, and sacrifice. God had a plan and she had to leave her feelings out of it that others would be saved and set free. God knew the whole time and had to sit back and watch from afar. God has a plan for each of us, but we must be willing and obedient. There was an anointing on Esther. But she had to come into the knowledge of it and come into the willingness of fulfilling God's plan on our lives.

This glory is what we have but we must be willing to endure the process and be obedient in order to receive the inheritance that God has set out for us to receive. But we cannot allow our image of beauty to become distorted by television programs and magazines instead of us understanding that beauty comes from within. It is not based upon make up and clothing but based on our faith and belief in God. Esther's beauty was far more than just her appearance. She had such a willingness to heed to instruction and listen yet conduct herself as herself and not of any other images that she seen. It was an inner beauty that was formed based on her path of life that was preordained by God that set her apart and formed her into this bold, confident, and obedient woman. This is what made the King so inquisitive about her and he found delighted in her presence that he inquired of her again. She had favor with the King. She didn't have fame or fortune. But she had favor that produced her purpose of existence in the Earth.

The enemy is fighting us on walking in obedience by surrendering our will over to the Father that we may receive His favor.

Esther was not consumed with the opportunity of the throne; she did not care or want it. There was a decree made by the King for the entire province. Then the Lord began to unveil the bigger picture that arose which was a massive genocide of her people. Then she probably realized even more that there was more to it than a throne but the saving of her people. Mordecai made this statement to her found in Esther 4:14 (AMP): And who knows whether you have attained royalty for such a time as this [and for this very purpose]?"

If we just began to conform our mind to His Word, then we can walk in His image which can order our steps in fulfilling His Purpose for our life just like in the story of Esther.

The enemy comes to steal, kill, and destroy. The devil wants to deceive and trick us by painting distorted images in our mind that robs us of our purpose and keeps us bound and not walking in freedom. Instead, we are led by these lies that he whispers in our ear about our imperfections and makes us doubt and fear. But we must not let fear keep us hostage especially when achieving our purpose, because your purpose is going to liberate you and restore others.

As I reflect in working towards my purpose, I can reflect and say thus far thank you Lord for the struggles, pain, and disappointments because they made me depend more on Him and gave me the strength to persevere on. Even when the devil would throw all that he could throw yet God's leading of His mighty hand kept me strong and I realized that no one else deserves or can take any glory. He also grants you the favor and spares His grace to get through every obstacle to accomplish the purpose for which God calls us to accomplish on the Earth. Through staying focused on the plan for which

God created us for will help us to not lean to the lies of the enemy and see that God created us for much more than to just simply exist.

As we continue to cruise through life, we will realize there is always this force (which is God) working on our behalf. He is always a very present help in the time of trouble. In the meantime, He is guiding us and shielding us from all hurt, harm, and danger. So many times, many people consider our lives to be lame and hopeless because they have not tapped into their own identity which is found in God.

In each of us, God has placed gifts on the inside of each of us that need to be unwrapped. These gifts known also as talents and natural abilities are characteristics that assist and guide us in carrying the light of God into every corner that exists today. But what the enemy wants to do is get us to fall prey to the standards of the world. He does not want us to create our world by speaking the Word of God, but to remain distracted by the cares of this world. This causes us to fall into sin by denying the power and neglecting our gifts within us which leads us to hide behind the mask; afraid to move forward. Therefore, we live a lie and are stifled by what people think, say, and believe. But, trying to live up to everyone's standards can be overwhelming at times because God shaped and molded us (like the potter's clay on a wheel) for a specific purpose.

I could imagine how Jesus must have felt. He was born as a child but didn't fit in. He was different but there was nothing He could do to prove that to anyone until the appointed time. He had a love for the things of God and loved to be amongst the wise (not a typical twelve-year-old child). He desired the things of God. He couldn't help it because God created Him for a specific purpose. This is like many of us. We have a call on our life to carry out an assignment that only we can accomplish through utilizing what He placed on the inside of us.

The way to walk in and fulfill this assignment for which we are created is to abide in His Word, abstaining from the world's devices yet becoming of one mind with Christ. Jesus did not succumb to the tactics of the enemy but remained true to himself and did not mind being set apart. We must carry on as such and not be afraid to be set apart but embrace it. This is not easy but if Jesus endured it then we can endure it too. He was tempted just like us yet without any sin. There was an obligation that He fulfilled and made up in His mind that no one or nothing was going to deter Him from that assignment. This is how we must be in today's world. There are so many distractions, temptations and evils that can dissuade us from carrying out our purpose or pursuing God. We need to be vigilant and alert, knowing that the devil is looking to kill, steal, and destroy. He wants to steal our hopes, aspirations and dreams. All of which were given to us so that we could help others and not just ourselves. Yet the world is built on greed, lust, and deception. Most people are doing everything for money, fame, and fortune instead of giving glory to God and worshipping Him only. But money is not the issue; it's when we make it our god instead of serving the one and true God.

This is where we go wrong today. Our hearts have turned away from God and focused more on our problems instead of turning to the problem solver. We decide to turn only to Him when our situation becomes intense and unbearable, then we start to pray and go to church to praise His name. We pick Him up and put Him down when we want to as if He is a toy. Will we ever wake up or will we keep wandering going in circles? Will we come to our senses and realize that God has more for us than mediocrity? Many are still confused and lost because they have become accustomed to living up to the world's standards for living a certain lifestyle. They continue to work in their own power and might; losing sight of The One who gave them the ability and gift in the first place. I bet this is a disgust in the nostrils of God. This is the reason why Lucifer was thrown out of heaven for stooping to the level of pride, and like him many of us are taking that same path and heading down a road that leads to destruction. It is the pride of man that causes their downfall. It can also cause one's heart to be hardened.

Sometimes we get so entangled in bondage that it is difficult to get out of it on our own. The only way is by God's providential help. It amazes me when some of us come out of desperate situations, yet we still end up turning our back on God and living any kind of way. When we know it had to be God to pull us out of the hole. Then we say, "God understands, and I still love Him," yet you don't because of all the other things you make a priority instead of Him. There is a day coming when we will all have to stand before the judgment seat. We shouldn't worry about what He will say to us because we will know that we lived a life before Him that is based on love and repentance, and worthy of the calling.

When living out His purpose for our lives we will realize that it is not worth losing our identity over the lies and disappointments of others. We must get unraveled and recognize that life is not just about ourselves but a greater picture that includes fulfilling our destiny to expose the lies of the enemy and come out with a testimony.

Prayer:

Lord, help me to reflect on my past as a steppingstone to my future and not a stumbling block. Lord, help me to take the time to thank you for not throwing me away but seeing more than what I see for my life. Thank you, Lord, for opening my eyes and facing who I am in the mirror, understanding that the old has passed away and behold You will do a new thing in me. Lord, I Embrace the past and prepare for my Future in You, in Jesus' Name.

Reflections

28

Chapter II

What Do I Do Now?

Everyone has a story to walk out and a journey to fulfill. The journey does not get easier, in fact it gets more challenging as you mature in your faith. It is shaping and molding us to become the best leaders God intended for us to be. So, we do not overlook the process or the mistakes of our past but embrace them knowing that they are making us into His image; therefore, we are not going to be easily dissuaded, rejected and disappointed but excited, uplifted and encouraged through these mistakes. We must believe that it is all working together for our good and for a bigger purpose. The wonderful thing is that our life has already been mapped out by God. We just need to walk it out.

A breaking point came in my life that tested my faith. Through this test made me see God clearer in my life and deepened my relationship with Him. It happened at a time when I was on my own and didn't have anyone around to rescue me from it all. To this day, I thank God for not intervening but for allowing me to see for myself the significance of having a relationship with Him all along.

Sometimes we are looking for someone to come to our rescue and bring us out of or up from the place where we are, not realizing that God is the only one that can rescue and restore us from our sin. Therefore, experiencing through the reality of life the power of our God to reveal how much he loves us by allowing us to come into the knowledge of the truth for ourselves.

We sometimes see and think of God as this mysterious image from a fairy tale created by man that paints a picture of Him being far away or from the land called far, far, far away land. We think that He is like a genie in a bottle and all we need to do is blink our eyes or clap our hands then things will just change. But this walk with Christ is built upon establishing our faith. Therefore, the only way for us to grow in this faith is through believing which is seeing Him for ourselves in our own situations that we experience in life. When we began to belief it is showing God that we trust that He is there and fully submitted and surrendered to His plan. He promised to never leave us or forsake us.

Through trusting Him, we are learning how to make the right decisions and not lean to our own understanding. Sometimes we can make wrong choices and turn away from Him. But when we repent and ask forgiveness it is wonderful to know that no matter how many times, we turn away He will receive us and remember our sins no more and help us to get back on the right track. He promised never to leave us or forsake us. It is us that get in the way and leave Him. He wants to do in our life Ephesians 3:20, paraphrasing "exceedingly and abundantly, above all we can ask or think." He also wants to protect and surround us with His angels to make sure we are safe from all the darts of the wicked one. For God so loved the world that He gave His only begotten Son that whosoever believeth on Him shall not perish but have everlasting life (John 3:16).

As Disciples of Christ, therefore we should share in that abundant life with Him so that others may see the fruit that we bare and be persuaded to live and serve the true and living God. When people see you, they should see a representation of Christ in the Earth and we should bear fruit such as peace, joy, patience, temperance, and most of all love. Through seeing and experiencing this fruit will make others thirsty and hungry for what it is like to have Christ. Therefore, this display that we show to others wherever we go is a great demonstration and witness of being a child of God. This display is what people around us should see and this will raise questions as well as spark interest in the minds and hearts of others; therefore, making the gospel message more appealing to all. Instead of chasing the world we should have others chasing after us to be more like Jesus. This is what the great commission was all about. He didn't want us to force our opinions and beliefs on others, but to just be like Him wherever we go. Then, it was left up to us to choose Christ.

Our main message was to not only be hearers of the Word of God but to be doers. In doing, others can see and then they will imitate and be. This is a part of our mission as Children of God to demonstrate Him by walking in love as we fulfill our purpose.

In serving out our purpose we are serving others and spreading love, it doesn't require you to become best of buddies and agree all the time with others but standing firm in the truth found in the Word of God. The commandment that remained was that you love regardless of how others may react to you or don't react at all.

When Jesus died on the cross, He knew everyone was not going to receive Him, yet He was still willing to die for all of us. His purpose was to redeem us from eternal damnation by being the ultimate sacrifice that we may inherit eternal life. He was that propitiation for us, the access in which we are redeemed from a life of death; and all we must do is repent, believe, confess, and accept Him as Lord and Savior. Christ didn't die for some people but for all who would receive Him. He is no respecter of persons. He desires for us to come into a covenant with Him so that we can inherit the abundant blessings of being kingdom citizens. This is the peace that we can have in Him, knowing we will not die in vain or live in vain but have that peace which passes all understanding.

Just like in my encounter as I ventured off to college on my own, I realized that I didn't really know him or believe as much as I thought I did. He had to allow me to really see the holes in my life and in my faith and how much that I needed Him. In seeing this, I began a relationship with God for myself and sought out God in a way that I never had. I began to see Him as a true Deliverer and Shepherd.

When pursuing our purpose, we should be anchored in our relationship with God. All it takes is for us to have our very own encounter with Him; then, it is up to us to listen, obey, trust and do or disengage, run away, disobey and hide.

A great example of someone who surrendered and obeyed God was Apostle Paul; his name at first was Saul and he was a murderer. He was finding errors with Jesus and killing those who followed Him. He was pursuing Christians to kill them. He was working against Him and was blinded by the authority of the kingdom in which he was serving at the time. Many were distraught by Christ teaching because he was sharing teachings that freed people from the law and were against tradition. Then Jesus was a threat because He was willing to go against the system. The Lord saw fit to use Saul. He struck him blind while on the Damascus Road. Saul had an encounter with Jesus that would change his life forever. God showed him that He was in control and Saul realized who was Lord that day and it changed him from a murderer to a preacher in three days. All it takes to change you forever is an encounter that overturns every doubt and gives you the unwavering faith that He is real. Paul began to share his encounter and experienced God in a new way. I am sure that while Paul was blind those three days that his eyes were truly becoming open and heart was growing tender to receive Him. Then his perception, knowledge, and understanding of Jesus changed and he was convinced that Jesus was real, and he set out to serve Him.

It is amazing how God takes the time to visit us on our Damascus Road Experience. He doesn't look at our faults and judges us but sees something greater on the inside of us. The entire time that we are on our journeys, He reveals to us that we can't do anything on our own; we need His help as we follow the purpose for which He ordained for us. He wants to offer us the deal of a lifetime. One that will change our lives forever and give us everlasting life. This includes having joy, peace, and the grace of God in our lives every day.

My Road to Damascus encounter was during college. Upon my arrival I had such excitement and zeal yet as I began to settle in, I felt alone and afraid. I began to experience and see a lot. I realized that it is not all the hype and felt a dire need to get back into a deeper relationship with Christ. Encounters that we have on the route of our purpose should push us towards God. This time of my life truly changed my whole perspective of God and deepened my relationship with Him that strengthened my faith forever.

As we progress in life, our relationship with God should deepen. I am reminded of this scripture in James 1:24: 2 My brethren, count it all joy when ye fall into divers temptations; 3 Knowing this, that the trying of your faith worketh patience. 4 But let patience have her perfect work, that ye may be perfect and entire, wanting nothing.

God is perfecting that which is in us that we exude a more excellent glory. We cannot stay the same. But should always be growing. I reminded that when we are babes in Christ, we drink milk. But as we mature, we began to eat the meat. This truly happened for me. But we need to think does He truly have my soul? Am I in a healthy relationship with Him? Am I stuck?

 As we go through encounters with Him, we began to see how He is omniscient and omnipotent. We don't see Him as just our Savior but our Healer, Provider and Deliverer. We get to see the many facets of Him. During different stages of our lives there are parts of Him that have such weight because of our season. As we keep living, we began to make room for Him as a priority and not second or last in our life. Therefore, not hiding or being ashamed of Him anymore but telling everyone the importance and need for God in your life.

It is critical today that you do not become religious; but that you establish a relationship with God for yourself. During my transitional season, I had to count the cost, observe my surroundings, and plan to either reconnect my relationship with God or die right there in my sin and waste the opportunity which was so very close to my door. As I continued this new journey, I realized how faithful and gracious God was to me. I thank Him for His grace that protected me when I didn't even see. I am grateful for God not allowing me to become a fool or getting swallowed up in my mess and pity; but was waiting patiently and ready to receive me back with loving arms again. Sometimes we make decisions that positions ourselves in awkward positions that were never intended for us to experience. But it is through these experiences that we find God and realize the power and faithfulness of our God.

At the end of Paul's Damascus Road journey, his life was never the same too. He was completely transformed.

Through that journey, he was able to experience and understand that Jesus was no longer some man but The Man. Paul's journey is the way that our lives can be carried out if we take the time to see and understand that only God can empower and help us. Jesus unveiled Himself in a way that can change our lives forever; but we need to be willing and obedient as well so that we can understand the need for a Savior. He is not a dictator, but a loving and gracious God who wants to add to you and not to take from you and desires for us to live a life that is full and fulfilling. But He doesn't force Himself on us but wants us to receive Him and accept Him then we can see and experience His benefits. He promised never to leave us or turn away from us but cannot keep what is promised if we turn away from Him. He is always willing if we are willing.

There will be times life throws us blows that the enemy uses to try to steal, kill, and destroy us and deter us from following Him. But through turning to Christ, by way of His Word, we can rise above those blows and overcome them one by one. By the end of the trial, you will know that it was only the grace and mercy of God that brought you through. But all the while God allows the tests to help grow your faith in those challenges, as your faith grows, you mature and climb to a new level and you rediscover God in a whole new way that expands your relationship with Him.

It was during my months away from home while at college, that I encountered unfamiliar territory that led me to seeking Him and helped me to see that I truly needed Him. I didn't feel comfortable at times and suddenly an alarm went off inside of my head. My spirit which was dark and dwindling awakened to the light. As I went towards the light, I felt free and could see clearly to hear and take heed to the voice of God again. It was in a situation at the time like that of Joseph. I had to flee from the very plight of mischief and a strong, hurricane-like temptation that was trying to swallow me up; yet God, sent his angels to rescue me out and restore breath into my nostrils.

When God turns the light on in your life, it is a way of escape for you and the best thing to do is flee from the very presence of evil and do not look back. At this time in my life my spiritual eyes reopened, my realization heightened to a great extent to the fact that I had almost been trapped by the enemy. I never would have imagined that someone who claimed to be so anointed, religiously attended church, worshipped and praised God like I did, filled with the Holy Spirit at 12, would ever be deceived and fall into all the traps that the enemy set for me. But I did and had to admit that there were some things in me lingering and needed to come out and how it happened subtly. It started with one standard being lowered and then another. Then the trick to conform and reflect a certain image that appeared to me was as popular. But all the while was being made a mockery out of and didn't at the time realize it. It happened subtly but my guard was down, and I didn't stay rooted and grounded. I didn't keep on my armor.

As I reflect on that time in my life, I know it was nothing but the grace of God that made a way of escape for me. But if you are not cautious and aware of the tactics of the enemy you too can get caught up in the traps that are set. The enemy has a job to steal, kill, and destroy. He will try to convince you to follow the crowd and lay aside your relationship with God. Instead of casting down those thoughts that are not good you began to give into those lies that are circling in your mind which breeds negativity and doubt. Also pacifying you, by saying phrases like "It (whatever your weakness is) that it's ok, just do it this one time, it won't hurt you." And his famous line, "You will not get caught." If you listen to these thoughts from the enemy, you will find yourself in places you would have never imagined;

knowing of God but the signal in your connection of your relationship with Him will weaken in being able to hear clearly and become disconnected eventually.

So, God tries to get your attention by allowing you to go through a valley experience or do it your own way that breaks you down and enables you to realize the significance of Christ in your life and internalize how nothing or no one else is greater than Him. After being released from the experience and being exposed to the outcome of what could have been and the magnitude of what could have been destroyed and may have been exposed because of what you went through and its effects. Then all you can do is thank God and serve Him because you should not be alive, in your right mind, or healthy.

Every day I look back and say "Lord, if it wasn't for your grace and mercy, I don't know where I would have ended up." Sometimes looking over your life, helps find what could have happened if He didn't hold back the enemy and then still used the situation to work out for your good (Rom.8:28). One can't help but to run, shout, leap and worship as hard and as loud as possible because of all that He has done. Just pause right now and began to think. For many of us, He kept back a premature death by allowing a bullet to miss our head or a vital organ, by ejecting us from the car just in time before the car engine blew up, or let's get real by not allowing the condom to break and transacting HIV or AIDS. There are plenty of other ways that God spares us. You even may have had those things to happen to people close to you and they were angels. Yet God saw fit to keep you alive and use you like He did Paul because He has a bigger purpose in mind for your life. Thank God for His grace and mercy!!!

Living outside of God's will is not a good feeling but is taking the chance of falling into those any of those things mentioned above every day. We are taking this precious gift of life and playing rushing roulette. In fact, it leaves you susceptible and vulnerable to all the evil plots and wicked devices the enemy uses to end our lives prematurely. For instance, there is nothing fun about having to be tested and receive results to find out you have a sexually transmitted disease that cannot be cured, having the police and caseworkers come to your house to retrieve your children due to being heavily addicted on alcohol and drugs that places them in danger of being hurt, neglected and abused, or if you are going to prison for life without parole, or if you are waking up next to live a job that you know you lied and cheated to get in order to live the American dream. Every day you are risking everything trying to live a false sense of success and appear in front of people like you have it all together. It is hard enough living in the will of God and having to face the challenges and tragedies of the world because the enemy is threatened by a Woman of God that made the Lord her King. But not living in His will places us in a position to not have any insurance coverage which is our inheritance that guarantees us redemption, restoration that includes and creates a fresh beginning as if nothing ever happened.

But as you keep doing your own thing it causes you to fall in the trap of hopelessness, depression, and insignificance which drives addictions and or mental illness that makes up a large percentage of women. This is not the will of God. He never intended for us to carry the weight alone. God came that we may have life and have it more abundantly. As we fulfill God's will we have to understand that the world is filled with temporal things but life with the Lord is never ending which means it lasts forever. Although the cares of this world exist and forms around us, it is a relationship with Christ that gives us hope and fill us with joy and peace that exceeds everything else in our lives as we hold fast to His hand. We should hold on to the fact that Jesus nailed everything already to the cross. Now we are to speak and walk as such in faith understanding no matter what we go through that we are victorious and overcomers. As it says in I John 4:4, Greater is He that is us than He that is in the world.

The peace and joy that you are searching for is found in a relationship with God. It is through that relationship with Him that we truly understand the significance of having Christ in our life and importance of having Him daily.

But when you are not connected to God it creates a path that is set for all kinds of unending attacks. They bring about confusion, destruction, and unwanted shame. Through not having a covering over your life, provides for unwelcomed visitors to walk into your life to contaminate your space. These unwanted visitors will dwell within your midst and sit down and take residence if you allow them to in your life. This is not how I would want to live my life and why a relationship with God is so needful. But it requires communication and trust on our part to build this relationship which requires sacrifice and surrendering.

A great illustration of the relationship that we need with God is that of a marital covenant, Christ is the bridegroom and we the church is His bride. Jesus is the way to the Father as we accept and confess Jesus as Lord, we gain access to reaching the Father. Jesus made the sacrifice for us that we can become joint heirs of Christ. So, we now have Christ living in us and it is our responsibility to bring glory to our Father in heaven by living a life that is pleasing unto Him.

When in a marital covenant, the two people (when saved and committed to God) understand that it is not to be taken lightly and they have roles to play within the marriage to ensure that it is fruitful and long lasting such as children and favor. It says in Proverbs 18:22 that He that findeth a wife finds a good thing and obtaineth favor from the Lord. We accept Christ, He already died, now we have an opportunity to walk into this covenant with Him.

In order to grow closer together you have to spend time with one another and get to know one another through the Word and then the relationship will flourish and grow this is how that in a marital covenant that the wife shows the husband her undying love by spending time getting to know what He likes and what He thinks. This is the way of our (church) relationship with Christ. Then we will desire more of Him and His will for our lives because we understand that He wants to ensure that we live the abundant life. Through getting to know our mates and spending time with him is the only way to endure and overcome in anything together. Well, God wants that same time and commitment with Him by meditating on His Word and being in His presence. This is how we can come to know Him and understand that it is His protection and covering that keeps us safe from all harm and danger. As we continue to abide in Him and Him abide in us, we can ask and pray for anything and it will be given. (John 15:7)

The Word of God is our map to experience the abundant life God promised us. As we are following that map, we are walking in His will and there is nothing like it because He truly desires for us to do greater works. Through God we have an opportunity to obtain everything we desire and more as well as live our dreams. But it requires us to be selfless, willing to sacrifice, and surrender which is not comfortable at times or easy to do to experience that abundant life.

When we are living outside of His will there are weights that we carry that limits us and blinders that keep us blinded from walking freely and living the abundant life which is found in the purpose of our existence. But the disconnection with God, can land us smack down in the middle of the enemy's territory. So, the main objective is to stay connected to God. He doesn't leave us, but we walk away from Him, we have a decision to make. The wonderful fact about God is that He loves us so much that He doesn't force us to be in a relationship with Him but gives us free will. He doesn't make us choose Him but leaves it up to us to need Him. When we tell God that we don't need Him it is like spitting in His face. It is also like telling the manufacturer of the vacuum that you don't need the manual. So, when the vacuum is malfunctioning the owner is helpless because it threw away the manual. In the same way, God is our manufacturer and the Word is the manual that will give us insight in how we work but He cannot help us because we refuse to receive His hedge around us; therefore, leaving us defenseless without any protection or guidance. This open gateway interferes with our decisions that leads to consistent mental break downs, low self-esteem, deep depression, and all kinds of phobias.

There is no money, fortune, or fame that can buy you healing when you are diagnosed with an incurable disease, and it is leaving you hopeless. The most dangerous place to be in is not having anyone to turn to in your darkest moments and having everything stripped away. But God never abandons you, unlike some people and everything else. We are still handed a choice to repent and turn back to Him. During these times without Him His plan for our life never changes but is available for us after surrendering over to Him. Hopefully it will not be too late. He is always faithful and prepared to pull us through our situation and rescue us out of every pit when we call on His name and repent of our sins. He is just waiting for you to accept Him, repent and turn away from your sin, and take heed to adhere to His voice. So, one day you can hear, "Well done thy good and faithful servant."

Prayer:

Lord, thank You for never giving up on me or leaving me. When I didn't have the strength to endure, you gave me the ability to press on and hold on it through it all. I am so thankful and grateful for all that You have done! I could never imagine what life would be like without you and I never want to experience that Oh Lord. For I need You! I hunger and thirst for You like the dear panteth for the waters. So, my soul panteth for you. I give my entire life over to You. Give me wisdom, discernment and knowledge to run this race so that it may bring You the Glory and Honor due unto Your name!

As I shared previously, in the first few years at college there came a dark cloud surrounding me and I realized that I desperately needed Him. I felt like I was losing my grip on life and I was so afraid. My fear was leading me downward on an irreversible path where any and everything came in to alter what God had for me. This was an awkward place to be in because I had never experienced this feeling before. Because you have never experienced a feeling, you don't know what you can do or where you will end up. If there was ever a time when I needed Him before, it was right then and there. I was at my lowest and that was when I had to rekindle my faith in God. The Jesus in me had to wake up. I had to turn the volume up on His Voice in my head and tune out the other voices. Courage rose up in me and fear released its hold on me because of the authority and power that lies within me. I was no longer bound but free because of the authority and the power of the Name of Jesus that lied within me. This is when my foundation became evident and the yoke of bondage was loosed from around my neck.

I was reminded of the scriptures of my childhood that my Mom and Dad gave me which was embedded in my heart that sprouted forth during difficult times. Such as I am the Head and not the tail, I am above and not beneath, I am more than a Conqueror. The Word of God says in Matthew 17:20 AMP,

> "Because of your little faith [your lack of trust and confidence in the power of God]; for I assure you and most solemnly say to you, if you have [living] faith the size of a mustard seed, you will say to this mountain, 'Move from here to there,' and [if it is God's will] it will move; and nothing will be impossible for you."

I recalled the scriptures of my youth, of who I am in Him; so, I started to quote them all and say them every day; If God be for me who can be against me?, I am fearfully and wonderfully made" Once I was no longer bound in chains, I regained my strength in the Word and my Savior reassured me that everything will work out, I began to pray and seek His face daily for direction early in the morning and fasting. I expressed to Him that I am ready to obey and be willing to do anything He wanted me to do and I would do it. Basically, the song came out, "I Am Yours Lord."

When I saw how my life was out of control and spiraling into a dark place, suddenly the light from heaven shined and God's grace and mercy lifted me out of the storm. I could not help but to serve Him wholeheartedly and serve Him the remaining years on that campus. It was His grace all along on my life that delivered me out of the pits that tried to destroy me by sending warnings. Then dispatching His angels to surround me and even delivering me from a mindset of being lost and in a confused state of being that led me down a misleading and not promising path that tried to alter my destiny.

The task of the enemy is to get us to forget who and whose we are in God. He wants to drag us down into a spiral spinning us all around so that we eventually lose our mind that will enable us from breaking free form the strongholds that tie us down and reaching the destiny of which God has predestined for us to fulfill for our lives. But the devil is a liar. As we stay in the will of God and deepen our connection by studying His Word, this will prevent us from falling into the holes that is set to take us down.

Many people will never understand your testimony, but there is a select group of people assigned to you that will be saved from heading down the same road. They need to hear your voice because it is going to grip their hearts and help them to rise out of the ashes and pursue the purpose they were created to fulfill on this Earth.

As you begin applying the Word of God to your situations in life, it shifts the attention away from the enemy and helps to draw attention to the Power of your God. It is like awakening from your trance causing the baby (vision, assignment) within you to start leaping again. There is no feeling like taking your power back and standing up against the lurking demons who are trying to choke you to death and intimidate you too and stop you from believing. It is in those moments that you realize that this was a spiritual attack that tried to take you out, but God already knew but needed you to wake up and see. Also, there were people assigned to you interceding on your behalf to pray for the restoration of your joy and peace and for your strength to be renewed like the eagles. Sometimes your faith is low and your connection with God is not strong. But God always raises people up on your behalf to pray for you because as the Bible says, "The fervent, effectual prayers of the righteous availeth much." There are many other moments in life that it is too good to be true that the prayers of the righteous were holding me up.

Now, I understand and realize more importantly how interceding for others can be the only source that is maintaining them when they are weak. Many times, we are so consumed with ourselves that we forget that there are other people who are in need of our help because we are so wrapped in our own problems that we forget we have a purpose which is our testimony; for as the Bible says in Revelation 12:11, "And they overcame and conquered him because of the blood of the Lamb and because of the word of their testimony, for they did not love their life and renounce their faith even when faced with death." Through knowing these scriptures is what frees us from feeling helpless, insignificant and hopeless.

In the end, I came to the realization that God really loves me. So, no matter what your past mistakes, failures or problems are God has a plan for His life and desires to use them for His Glory. He does not count or hold against you anything from the past; instead, He places them in the sea of forgetfulness and remembers them no more. But many times, we hold on to them instead of letting them go and it takes hardships and setbacks in life to help us see that God's intentions for us is to never harm us but to bless us. But trusting in Him with our whole heart and not leaning to our own understanding is the key to receiving the blessings.

I am reminded of the story in the Bible of the woman at the well, John4:7, who had an encounter with Jesus Christ that changed her and her family's life forever. She came for water but left the well never to quench from thirst again. Jesus presented her with an opportunity that could not be resisted. She was searching for something that could not be fulfilled through a man. She instantly was filled with the agape love of Jesus and her life was made whole again. She was also willing to receive what Jesus had to offer that made a big difference. Jesus saw something missing, offered her salvation to help overcome this pattern, and then she was willing to receive.

This is the type of encounter that everyone should have and understand because it is a gift available to all mankind to grant them peace and joy. It fulfills every need that the Heavenly Father desires to give to each one of His children. He is sitting and waiting to become the lover of our souls and the captain of our ships. Yet, many are not willing to admit and surrender it all over to Him; instead they try to do everything on their own power and in their own might. Many times, we think we know what is always best for us. We fail to seek out our Creator who made us, and all we need to do is connect to Him to find our purpose then everything else will work for us. All we need to do is believe then we can repent, turn, and confess that He is Lord and He will cleanse us and make us whole in every area of our lives. He did the ultimate sacrifice which was reconciled us back to God and gave us a new start. The sin that Adam and Eve committed would not hold us hostage and living under the old law, but Christ made us free.

Here is a simple Prayer that you can say:

> Lord, come into my life. I need your help. I realize that this is not the life I want to live. I desire your Son to live within me that I may live a free and abundant life in Him. Forgive me, Lord, for all of my sins. Wash me and cleanse me in your precious blood. Create within me a clean heart and fill me up again with your Spirit. I need you, Lord, and I desire you more than anything else.

After you pray this simple prayer, just sit in His presence and let Him fill you up. If you need a refilling of the Holy Spirit this is the time to ask Him and or to ask the Holy Spirit to speak to you. The wonderful thing about Jesus is that He provided help for us through the Holy Spirit (our helper and comforter) to function on this Earth. As we grow deeper in our relationship with God, He fills us up with more of His wisdom, knowledge and understanding so that we may prosper in all that we do, even as our soul prospers. Then as we delight in Him our desires intertwine that He can pour out on us more than we can ask or think.

As we continue to delight in Him, more of Him shines through us and we exemplify His beauty by allowing Him to work through us in the Earth. We are His workmanship. He is the potter and we are the clay. He created us knowing the very hairs upon our heads, our downsitting and uprising, desires, gifts, and thoughts. But reminds us that His ways are higher than ours and His thoughts are higher than our thoughts. He had an assignment in mind when He created each of us whether we choose good or evil. God does things strategically and His ultimate plan is to draw all men to Him; however, He is aware that not all will accept and follow Him. Yet God uses all things big and small as an example of His glory for example, the beauty of conceiving twins in the same womb, to bring us to an understanding of the vastness of His nature and the vastness of His creation. That is why living day in and day out without finding your true purpose is vanity. True happiness is found in fulfilling one's true purpose which you were specifically designed for by God to complete. A job is a task that can be daunting unless it is a part of your passion. If your job is a passion that is not daunting and yet you forget to clock out, then it is linked to your purpose. It can be used as a preparation tool, reference and or training to assist you in completing your purpose that does not bring about sorrow. But, having a relationship with God provides the ultimate fulfillment and gives us hope and joy of knowing that you have a greater purpose for living. So, although you may have a job or be in a place that is not your purpose, and you are pursuing your purpose, God will give you the strength and power to get through it. Therefore, giving clarity, a job can be an assignment from God that allows for the pleasure to serve without it even feeling like work, yet it is not your passion or purpose for which He specifically designed for you.

But, outside of God we are not led by our passions, but skills and educational training and we want God to ride along with our plan. But this choice of separating God out of our lives leaves us feeling extremely tired and frustrated. Therefore, lacking the joy and peace that we truly find when we are fulfilling our hobbies. They are forms of relaxation that we find pleasurable and use as an outlet but can be harmful at times. It is not until we acknowledge God and make Him our priority that we find the ultimate peace and rest. When you reach that breaking point, you will seek out what drives you or brings you the most pleasure. This can either lead you down the wrong path or it can lead you to seek God. Again, there is peace which passes all understanding which only comes through seeking a relationship with God. He is the creator of all things and when we tap into Him, we can truly know and experience who He created us to be and our specific purpose for which we were created to fulfill on this Earth. Our ultimate purpose is to be witnesses and live for Christ but what is the way He gave it to you to do so.

To live out that dream deep down inside is what everyone truly desires. This is the purpose for which I am talking about. Yet, many times we are so consumed with the cares of life that we overlook or forget all about the dream. But this is a desire that was implanted in you since you were a baby. It is through your dream that you are reacquainted with your Creator; the One who gives you the ability to live that dream out. As you seek God, you will begin to fall in love with Him and gain a sense of living beyond a job or bills and business but of significance.

I want this book to help you realize that your life is significant. Hopefully you will discover it and will find a way to reignite some excitement in living life and zeal for living. A way to start is to spend time with yourself and write down your natural born gifts and passions that makes you unique and special. Then, you will begin to find your drive to keep living and keep going because it is your purpose of existence. This is the best feeling in the world. It is the reason to get up and look forward to every morning. There is no money that can buy such happiness or bring such joy. You can only gain it and keep that peace and joy is by pursuing God. He is the hub in the middle of a wheel which keeps you going in fulfilling your purpose when it gets challenging.

Many people in the world are searching, and I believe that the liquor stores and hospitals would not be as full if there were more people seeking their purpose and fulfilling their purpose. But they need to be connected to the Father in order to even see purpose. It is through your calling that you find your place in the world and are able understand how valuable you are to Him. He created you as a kingdom citizen to be bright lights that shines amid darkness. But how do you go about doing this in the Earth?

God allowed the sperm from the father to find the egg of the mother that came about to form a fetus that was in the womb of a woman. The amazing story of biology is that there are millions of sperm but only one finds its way through the fallopian tubes to connect with an egg that causes the fetus to be created. Therefore, all of us were strategically assigned to make it in order to carry out an assignment here on the Earth for God. It is up to us as individuals to tap into our gifts and seek God for a way we can fulfill those assignments. We have on our life. We are all a part of God's workmanship created to be a representation of Christ in the Earth so that we may reach all people for His glory.

Prayer of Thanksgiving:

Lord, thank you that I made it through my Mother's Womb. I know that You have a specific plan for my life, and I intend with Your help to carry out. Lord, guide me and give me Your wisdom on how I can fulfill this purpose on my life. Lord, I don't want to be like other people but what You created me to be. Mold me and shape me in Your image as I go out and pursue this passion, I have on my life, in Jesus' Name.

Reflections

Chapter III

How Do I Break Free?

In pursuing your dream that He has instilled in you before the foundations of the world, you will encounter challenges of different magnitudes. These challenges can hinder you from walking boldly in what God has called to do. But you must not withdraw under pressure or freeze in the middle of the crises; instead, you should hold and just trust God until He delivers you out. This will not be easy, but it will strengthen your faith and starve your doubts. While you are learning how to trust Him, you will be led to pray and fast which causes you to be more sensitive to His Spirit and draw closer to Him to gradually get through your crises. If you do not learn how to trust God by believing in Him wholeheartedly then the cares of life will consume you and become weights that will turn into strongholds that will keep you bound. It is best to let them go and let God in order to receive your healing and be set free. By resting in the Father and confiding in Him for every problem you are carrying can eliminate stress and negativity which places you on a road of recovery.

As you continue to progress on this road to recovery, the challenges you face may not impact you the same because of the working of your faith. But they continue to come at different angles trying to pull you down and you will experience feelings of regret, failure and sorrow because in this world we will face tribulation and trials. But it is all in how we look at them and attack them which must be through the Word of God. At times these trials can become overwhelming and unbearable; but this is when you must dive in the Word, reflect on testimonies and meditate on scriptures like Psalms 107:2.

Then God will strengthen you with the ability to walk with confidence and assurance in God that you never thought existed. Sometimes your trials will make you doubt and waver in your faith, but you must continue to pick up the Word. Remember that the darts will form but will not take you out because God has already made the ultimate sacrifice of His Son who carried all our sins and took the keys of death that we may have Eternal Life. But you must not give the darts more power than the Word of God! Remember you are surrounded by angels to keep you safe from all harm. God will also through His Word provide you with the wisdom and knowledge needed to handle them all. Therefore, you don't have to worry or walk around in fear, because God has already given you the victory. We need to learn how to rest in the arms of our loving Father, acknowledging that these trials are not trying to break us down but to build us up. God allows them to help us sharpen our faith and build up our resilience to the devil and flee from all kinds of temptation. Therefore, giving us the ability to gain back our authority and serve notice on the devil to understand that it doesn't matter what he throws but that God is the one and true living God.

It is the challenges that show us our weaknesses and builds our strengths. This is one of the ways that we can grow. They can bring a side of us that we don't even know is present in us. And, although we look at our challenges as difficult and uncomfortable, they are working a greater work in us such as patience, longsuffering, meekness, and kindness. This is all for the perfecting of us and makes us wiser, better and stronger to fulfill His purpose for our lives.

As I touched on in chapter one, a great illustration of how challenges that we can consider hiccups or less fortunate incidences that are unpredictable and not based on any fault from our own decision is in the book of Esther. Esther (who was also known as Hadassah) didn't know that her parents' death and unfortunate events in her life would all work together to be a part of a greater purpose in the end; positioning her to be seated at one of the highest places in the kingdom. She probably would never have imagined being in that seat when she was little. But she had to remain faithful and obedient to get there.

There are many who never thought that their lives would become as beautiful as Esther's; but her story portrays how God can take an ugly beginning and turn it into the most beautiful ending. It is just a matter of trusting and remaining obedient to His Word that we can fulfill and reach our destiny. Esther's story is also a reminder that fulfilling our assignment takes more than our beauty; it is humility and a willingness to incline to Godly counsel and maintain a connection with the Almighty who is more than capable of rewriting our story. Often, it is while we are pursuing our own plans that we realize that it would not be as hard to achieve them if we put our whole life in the Master's Hands.

His thoughts are higher than our thoughts, His ways are higher than our ways, His plans are bigger than our plans, and He is over all and knows all; therefore, His Word outweighs everything. Once we settle in our hearts and mind that His Word is first and last in our lives then it is easy to discover and enjoy the path that was already predestined for us.

But, many of us are wavering in our faith and unable to fully trust in God which leaves us stressed and depressed because we are unstable. When we are not strong in our Faith then any and everything can shake us. It is much like a vacuum cleaner that is not working properly, and the owner of the vacuum is not taking the time to read the manual thoroughly to see how to work it properly so that it can fulfill its use. God doesn't want us to carry weight that He sent His Son to carry for us; instead, He wants us to seize the gift of salvation through His Son which gives us ownership as sons and daughters to the throne of heaven. He sent His son to die that we may live a life free of all manner of sicknesses, diseases and cares of the world. But we must accept Him as Lord to receive our healing and breakthrough.

Jesus' death was the ultimate sacrifice that granted us our freedom from sin and redemption for us all in the

Kingdom that we may live a life that never ends. But the world is filled with the appearance of evil. People are denying the power within and searching for peace, love and joy in everything but God; which all leads to suffering, pain and hatred. It is the responsibility of every believer of Christ to be the salt of the Earth and the light of the world. In order to demonstrate this light, our walk should be confident, bold, and honest before others that they may be compelled to hear and wonder about our daily joy and peace.

We are the reflection of Christ in this world. He now lives in us. Therefore, we have the responsibility to live a life that is surrendered over to Him but, at times being like Him will be tested. You will feel like is this worth it or is this what you signed up for. It will seem like everyone is out to get you or that nothing is working for you. But, when you shake off the pressure and do not let it affect you, then you will realize that this is what you always dreamed of and anything worth having is worth fighting for. While we are on this Earth, the enemy will not stop trying to kill us; but God has given us the right to choose. It is like choosing our destiny or a life full of torment and running.

When you first get saved, you are so excited and elated and you may have thought everything was going to be great and fall into place. Almost like God was a genie in a bottle, and you were not going to face anything else bad in your life; however, this is not the full meaning of Salvation. It is a guarantee that if we heed to the Word of God then He can assure us that we will always have someone working on our behalf behind the scenes of the good, bad and ugly in our lives. All of this that we are doing is transforming our minds to conform to His image and conform to the demeanor of a champion that overcomes all obstacles by casting down any thoughts that are not aligned with the Word of God.

As you grow older, you realize that the dreams of your youth are more of a fairytale than reality. In life there are unexpected curves that can totally shake you in your boots, your spouse decides to commit adultery with someone close to you or a relative, your finances hit rock bottom and you are working three jobs at once, and your health declines quickly or disease consuming every organ in your body that doctors are baffled and don't know what to do. If you live on this Earth long enough, life can take you on some curves. This is not to say that life will always be miserable or disappointing but there will be challenges that can break you down and make you frustrated when things totally take a spin in the wrong direction. However, it is in those moments when you realize that living this life alone is not worth it. It is going to take the power of God and His strength to carry you through some situations for as the Bible says in Ephesians 6:12, "We wrestle not against flesh and blood but principalities and spiritual wickedness in high places." This is not a fight to handle with fists but a fight in the spirit realm. It takes the help of the greater one to direct you in the right direction emotionally and spiritually. This is when you should place your full confidence and trust in God to guide you. He is the only one that is more than capable and dependable on in this life to bring you through anything. In Him, you can abide and trust in forever. His word says in Proverbs 3:5-6, "Trust in the Lord with all your heart and lean not to your own understanding and in all thy ways acknowledge Him and He will direct your path."

As you continue to go through life's journey, I learned what it means trust in God by surrendering over my will. My surrendering allowed me to enter His peace and stay filled with joy regardless of what is happening in my life. Now I can confidently pursue my goals and live out my dreams because I see that life is worth living. It is through God that I realize He will never leave nor forsake you and will keep your mind and cover all your wrongs. In pursuing God, it will not be easy, and things may appear not to fall into place but Romans 8:28 says, that all things work together for the good of them that love God and are called according to His purpose. Also, we must continually speak what we desire and believe for it to come into existence because as the Bible clearly states, "Life and death are in the power of the tongue." God gave us the ability create our world by speaking it into existence if we are committed to Him, therefore we have an opportunity to choose whom we will serve then how we will carry out our lives on this Earth.

Since we have the right to choose, we cannot get upset when things do not go the way we planned. So, we need to conduct a self-evaluation to determine whether we are seeking our own will or His. This requires transparency and a letting go of our will. Then we can begin to reap all the promises God intended for us from the beginning of creation. This can be challenging for us to do because it requires a life full of sacrifices and selflessness in a world that is full of greed, selfishness, deception, lust, coveting, and backbiting. God desires to give us peace, joy and pleasures forever more but not with us living apart from Him. For what God gives

He adds no sorrow with it. As the Bible says, "His will is for us to prosper and be in good health even as our soul prospers." But seeking other things before Him makes them idols, therefore turning our worship away from God and putting them in the wrong direction by doing things in our own might which can make us fall into pride. Therefore, making it appear as if we know more than God. But all glory and praises should go to God because it is, He who gave us the power to obtain wealth. The gifts that we have and possess are all given to us from our existence in the womb. But how we use them is left on us.

If we really desire to be successful in this life, it is by seeking first the kingdom of God and His righteousness and all those other things will be added. God doesn't want us living a life of sorrow, but this happens when we don't depend on God. Instead, we want to do it in our own power, and might which can lead to burnout, neglect, sickness, and hopelessness. This is how some people live, they create a fantasy lifestyle but do not show the negative effects of such a lifestyle. Many are left feeling overwhelmed and burned out from trying to please the world because their soul is not at rest. Everything that glitters is not gold.

It is important to stay true to what you believe and be firm on that which is true for there is only one way to God but many false teachers. In pursuing a relationship with God, many will taint it by painting a picture of how slave owners used it to bind slaves and other religions used it to portray Jesus as a prophet using their own theology that fits their doctrine and not examining the truth . But do not get drawn into those discussions but let them see your walk. Many do not want to sacrifice and walk alone on this narrow path with God. They would rather live carelessly instead of fulfilling the destiny of what He predestined for them to do.

As the Bible says, "There is a way that seemeth right to man but can lead to destruction." Through seeking God, you can find everything you need. By maintaining an open and clear line of communication with Him, you can hear His voice, and not follow the voice of a stranger. Abiding in Him and Him in you is vital to thriving in God. Also, through a consistent prayer life, one can discern when it is Him speaking and when it is them speaking. When building a relationship with God, there are answers we may receive such as yay, nay, or nothing at all. We must learn how to endure and wait. He may not respond or come through when we want or at the time, but He will come through. The Bible also says, "His ways are not our ways nor His thoughts our thoughts." All that He does and says is for the working and testing of our faith in Him.

It may appear at times that God is hurting us or doesn't care about us while all the while he is positioning, perfecting and creating within us His perfect will. He allows the story to appear or get worse to form a platform and give you a testimony in front of your entire family, coworkers and friends so that they all will witness that He is real and is very present in our lives today. It is only through a strong relationship and constant communication of prayer with Him that you can connect and understand your purpose.

In many instances, we can get complacent living job to job and working for others instead of taking a leap of faith and walking into the God-given purpose that was grafted into our veins and hearts before the foundations of the world. We often stay stuck due to fear, lack of self-confidence or walking away from God. We have the opportunity of a lifetime to fulfill our dreams or find the will of God for our lives, but we get so consumed with the world. We create platforms outside of His will instead of building a strong foundation in God. But, when we surrender, He can step in and redirect us by putting us back on schedule with events through an alternative route orchestrating our steps to place us on a path to our destiny. But it is up to us whether, we are going to take the road that is set for up for us or for a less promising future; for we must walk by faith and not by sight.

The Word of God contains important instructions of what God has given to us for what God has promised us. We should utilize this opportunity of life to bring Him glory. It is easy to become a victim instead of walking as a victor. It is up to us to make sure to stay connected to Him through a relationship to remind us of who we are in Him. He told us that we are, "The head and not the tail, above only and not beneath" (Deuteronomy 28:13). We are children of the Most High God.

Reflecting on the story of Esther, her cousin did not raise her to be a victim. And although she was raised by her cousin and not by her parents, she did not misuse her past but kept it in perspective yet did not fall into a pit of defeat. She chose not to use her upbringing as an excuse and become a victim of it, but she relied on the teachings of the faith for which she was raised by her cousin. God used Esther's background to remind us that He still has a plan no matter how horrific your past to share with those of us who would read about her today that He can make even our unlikely and unthinkable history into the most famous and unforgettable stories.

Esther's story serves to rule out any excuses in pursuing your destiny or pressing through the disappointments or our very own secrets that keep us bound. Esther did not have it all and the conditions were not comfortable for her in the beginning of her life. Yet in the eyes of man, she was not the most likely candidate to become the next Queen. In fact, she was probably the least likely candidate on the list. Throughout the Bible there are many other stories and scriptures that attest to the fact that God doesn't look on the outward appearance of man or the resume but instead he looks at the heart. I am reminded of the story of David. When Samuel went searching for the next King and arrived at Jesse's house, Jesse brought forth his appealing sons; those whose physical appearance and stature fit that of a King. But, none of them carried the Kingly anointing of God. Instead, Samuel asked if there was another son. When the youngest son, David, came forth he was ruddy and little; yet handsome, he was the one that had the anointing to be the next King. Again, man looks on the outward appearance, but God looks at the heart. David was known as a man after God's own heart. Even as He matured and made a mistake he repented. He truly loved God. It is easy to get consumed in self, become defeated from looking back at your past failures and mistakes, and end up turning away from your destined path. But this is the trick of the enemy whose main objective is to deter man from pursuing God. We must remain consistent and stay faithful through it all.

The enemy can use manipulation and get us far from God. In these valley moments, deception can also lead us to think that we can never get back to God. We cannot believe this lie. But apart from the tricks of the enemy therefore, it is important to feast and drink upon the living water daily. Temptation will never stop as long as we live. It takes a consistent, daily regimen of meditating and indulging in His presence to help maintain a strong relationship with Jesus Christ. This will restrain one from getting caught up in worldly views and losing sight of God's purpose. By focusing back on God, we come to realize what the devil offers us and nowhere to compare to God's plan. We all are here today (believers and non-believers) to come into the Kingdom for such a time as this. Either way God has a plan and a purpose for everything under the sun (whether it is good or bad) because "The Earth is the Lord's and the fullness thereof" (1 Corinthians 10:26).

There are some of us who are still lost looking for our purpose in life. But some of us do not understand that it is all tangled up in God. It appears wonderful to land a career and obtain nice objects in life and fall into the norm; but there are some of us who know that there are bigger and better things in store for us. Those objects cannot give us peace. Instead God's purpose calls us in the midnight hour and wakes us up early in the morning. It is God tugging at our hearts; waiting for us to walk out the calling that is deep within. Staying wrapped up in Him will take you places you could never imagine; these places are unbelievable and so grandeur. These places will open to you of such great magnitude that you will not believe is true. Thereby revealing to everyone how merciful and gracious He is to those who diligently seek Him. If we just trust Him and take Him at His Word, then we can be a part of a great masterpiece that is molded and shaped to form a picture of Him in the Earth.

Through repentance, confession, dedication, and determination, we can seize everything God has destined for us to receive in His Word. When we commit our lives, He will perform a great work in us and finish it because He wants us to live a plentiful life for Him that is filled with purpose and peace. So that the Earth can experience another part of Him in the Earth. We are an outward expression of Him.

There is not a place that God is not there. He wants to use us to take the Word to go to the uttermost parts of the Earth. The way that this gets accomplished is through us surrendering over our lives and giving Him access to work through us. But just as much as God wants to get His kingdom agenda done, there is an enemy who will not let up. He keeps fighting to deter and detach us from the will of God. He doesn't want us to discover who we really are and tap into the gift God has placed within us because he knows we will become a threat to his kingdom.

We all are a threat to the enemy once we commit our lives to God. But we must understand that no weapon formed against us shall prosper. God's angels are protecting and covering us in His blood. As soon as doubt and negative thoughts arise, we should cast them down. God has given us power, love and a sound mind to take our lives back; we must forget those things that are behind and pressing toward the prize of the high calling which is in Christ Jesus (Philippians 3:12-14). Hopefully, your eyes are open, and your ears are attentive to all that God wants to do for you, you know by now that there is no one or nothing that can fill the void of Jesus. Some things may appear to work for a moment, but at the end of the day it is only Jesus that can give you the unending hope, joy, and peace you need to walk out your life every day.

I come to discover that the key to living this abundant life is through surrendering our will over to His which allows God to work through us and mold and shape us into His image in us. The Word of God gives me the motivation to live everyday with purpose knowing that it does not take the accolades of others to keep me on the right path; but all I need is Him more and more to lead and guide me along the way for He is a shelter and defense in times of storm. During times of loneliness and confusion, he reminds me that He will never leave me. He reminds us that we can do all things through Him who strengthens me. It is at my lowest that His Word resounds, "Greater is He that is in you than He that is in the world" (I John 4:4). Then He continues to remind us that, "Before I formed you in your mother's womb, I knew you" (Jeremiah 1:5). And in another passage, He says, "For who knows that you were created for such a time as this?" (Esther 4:14). Therefore, what great delight and pleasure it is to serve such a powerful and loving God; to offer back to Him our lives. This is the least we could do in exchange of a promising future that is filled with purpose and filled with unending blessings that He bestows upon us daily.

Prayer:

Lord, thank you for me accepting what I can't change and embracing the changes I need to make. Help me not to be consumed about the cares in the world that I forget what is most important. Lord, give me the strength to serve and have boldness to stand for what is right in life. Help me not to be consume with worry or fear that I abort the mission for which You have sent me here. Lord, I surrender my will over to You and trust that You will pull me through. Not my will but thy will be done, in Jesus' Name.

Reflections

82

Contact Information

To inquire about Melody Saunders speaking, ministering, or doing book signings and discussions at your event, send an email to:

etqwintlnetwork@gmail.com